BROTHER, TELL ME YOUR LIFE STORY

A guided journal filled with questions for brothers to answer for their siblings.

Brother, Tell Me Your Life Story

Copyright © 2019 by Jean Lee

Cover Design by Jean Lee

This book is for:

_____
_____
_____

What is your full name and birthday? Where were you born (city, state, and hospital)? Do you know your birth stats (time, weight, height)? Any interesting stories you've been told about the day you were born?

DATE:

Where are you in the birth order of siblings? Do you remember anything about the days your siblings were born?

DATE:

Which sibling were you closest to growing up? Do you remember
any of the games and toys we played with together as kids?

DATE:

Who are some of your favorite relatives?
Do you have any special memories of time spent with them?

DATE:

Did you know our grandparents or great-grandparents?
Tell me any special memories you have of them.

DATE:

What were the names of the schools you attended and what cities were they in? Did you graduate from high school? College?

DATE:

What were your favorite subjects in school?
Which subjects did you hate?
What were your grades like?

DATE:

What were your hobbies and interests as a child?
What hobbies and interests do you have today?

DATE:

Did you participate in any activities such as sports or music? Did you attend the school dances? Were you in any plays or concerts?

What is your best memory from childhood?
What is your worst? Would you say you had
a good childhood or a bad one?

List all of the jobs you've had throughout your life.
Which was your favorite? Which was your least favorite? Do you
remember how much money you made at each?

What was your first car? Do you remember how much you paid for it? What was the best car you've had in your life? Which was the worst? What is your dream car?

DATE:

Do you have any specific memories of me
or our other siblings from childhood?

_____

_____

_____

_____

_____

_____

_____

_____

_____

_____

_____

_____

DATE:

Tell me about your romantic relationships (if you want to)!
Who have you dated? Marriages? Divorces?

Tell me about all of the homes you've lived in.
Which was your favorite? Which one was the worst?
Describe your dream home.

Tell me what life was like for you in your 20's.
Were you happy?

DATE:

Tell me what life was like for you in your 30's.
Were you happy?

DATE:

Tell me what life was like for you in your 40's.
Were you happy?

DATE:

What were your favorite meals growing up?
Is there anything our parents served that you hated?
What is your favorite food today?
What is your favorite restaurant?

DATE:

What was your favorite type of music growing up?
What is your favorite song of all time?
Who is your favorite singer or band of all time?
Have you been to any concerts?

Do you enjoy reading?
What authors and/or books are your favorites?
Do you like to read newspapers and/or magazines?
If so, which titles?

DATE:

What were your favorite radio and/or television shows growing up?
Which are your all-time favorites? Who is your favorite TV actor or
actress? What is your current favorite television show?

Do you like to watch sports? If so, which ones?
Which teams are your favorite?
Who is your favorite athlete?
Have you ever attended a game in person?

DATE:

Tell me about your favorites.
Favorite color? Favorite season?
Favorite time of day? Favorite ice cream flavor?
Favorite number? Favorite flower?

What is your proudest accomplishment in life?
What is your biggest regret? If you could go back in time and
change anything, what would it be?

DATE:

Do you like animals?
Tell me about all of the pets you've had.
Do you prefer dogs or cats?

DATE:

Tell me about any memorable birthdays you've had.
What is the best birthday gift you've ever been given?
What flavor of birthday cake is your favorite?

DATE:

Did you serve in the military?
Is so, when and what branch?
Did you serve overseas? Did you see battle?
Did you receive any medals?
Who was your best military buddy?

Did you attend church growing up?
Were you baptized?
What religion do you identify with today?

DATE:

What was your most memorable Christmas?
What is the best present you've ever received?
What is the best present you've ever given?

Have you taken a lot of vacations during your life?
What was the best vacation you've ever been on?
The worst? Where would you still like to travel to?

DATE:

List all of the states you've visited.
List all of the countries you've been to.
Is there anywhere you'd like to visit that
you haven't been to yet?

DATE:

Do you remember what you wanted to be when you grew up?
Do you wish you had pursued a different career?

DATE:

Tell me about your health.
Do you remember being sick as a child?
What health problems are you facing today?

Have you ever ridden a train?
Flown in an airplane?
Been in a boat or on a helicopter?
Which did you prefer?

DATE:

What items have you collected over the years?
Do you still have your collections?
Are you collecting anything these days?

DATE:

What is your idea of the perfect day?
Where would you go? What would the weather be like?
What would you eat? Who would be with you?

DATE:

What was the best day of your life?
What was the worst day of your life?

DATE:

How would you like people to remember you?
What would you like to be known for?

What traditions have you passed on
to your family that you got from our parents?
What traditions have you given up?

DATE:

What is the most significant world event that you've lived through?
Has it had a lasting impact of your life?

DATE:

Do you have any bad habits that you wish you could break? Have people told you that you have a bad habit that you don't believe you actually have?

Do you like to go shopping?
What is your favorite store?
What types of things do you hate to shop for?

DATE:

Do you like to cook or bake?
Any special dishes that you love to prepare?

Have you ever been camping?
Have you ever ridden a horse?
Swam in a lake or in the ocean?

DATE:

Have you ever met anyone famous
or had a close brush with a celebrity?

What is your biggest fear?
Are there fears you had when you
were younger that you've overcome?

DATE:

What rules did our parents have for us as children?
Do you remember how we were punished?

What is your most embarrassing memory as a child?
What is the most embarrassing
thing you've experienced as an adult?

DATE:

What was your most prized childhood possession?
Do you still have it?
What is your most prized possession today?

DATE:

What political party to you belong to?
How many Presidents have you voted for?

DATE:

Do you remember any shared Christmas
presents we received as kids?
What kinds of things were in our Christmas stockings?

What Christmas traditions from our childhood
have you carried over into adulthood?

DATE:

Which is your favorite season:
Winter, Spring, Summer, or Fall?
Which is your least favorite?
Do you prefer warm or cold weather?

What do you remember about our childhood Thanksgivings?
What traditions have you carried over into your adulthood?
As for turkey, do you prefer white or dark meat?
Pumpkin, apple or pecan pie?

Did you have a role model or mentor growing up?
Did you have any favorite teachers or coaches?

DATE:

Do you remember having nightmares as a child?
Do you have them as an adult?
Have you ever had any recurring dreams?

Are you superstitious, such as not letting a black cat cross your path, not walking under ladders, not breaking a mirror, or throwing salt over your shoulder?
Do you have a lucky number? A lucky charm?

Have you ever been through a natural disaster such as a flood, tornado, or earthquake? Have you ever experienced an excessive heat wave or a massive snow storm? Do you like thunderstorms?

DATE:

Do you have any memories of Valentine's Day from when you were a child? What has been your favorite Valentine's Day as an adult?

DATE:

Do you keep in touch with any of your childhood friends?
Have you attended any class reunions?
If you did, were they fun? If you didn't go, why not?

DATE:

What chores did you have as a child?
Were they different from mine?
Did you receive an allowance?

Have you had your wisdom teeth removed?
How about your appendix? Tonsils?
What surgeries have you had?

DATE:

What do you remember from our family Easter celebrations?
Do you remember if we dyed and hunted for eggs?
What did the Easter Bunny put in our baskets?

DATE:

What was your favorite piece of playground equipment
as a child? Did you have a fort or secret hiding place?
Did we play outside together?

DATE:

Did you have any nicknames growing up?
Were you ever teased or picked on in school?

DATE:

What memories do you have from our family's summer vacations?
Where was your favorite place we went?

DATE:

Have you ever been ice skating?
Roller skating? Skiing?
Do you know how to swim?

DATE:

What is the most trouble you ever got into as a child?
What punishments did our parents hand out to you?
Did you ever get in trouble at a job?

DATE:

Have you ever been in a physical fight?
What's the worst argument you've ever had with someone?

Did you go to the school dances in junior high and high school?
What about the football and basketball games?

DATE:

Do you remember what Halloween was like when we were kids?
Did we ever trick-or-treat together?
Do you remember any of the costumes you wore?

DATE: _____

What were your favorite candies as a child? Do you remember
where you bought candy and how much it cost?
What is your favorite candy now?

_____

_____

_____

_____

_____

_____

_____

_____

_____

_____

_____

_____

Have you had a favorite boss? A boss you couldn't stand?
Did you get along with your co-workers?
Was there someone you worked with who you really disliked?

DATE:

What is the best part of being a brother? The hardest?

DATE:

What has been your greatest achievement in life?
What has been your biggest regret?

DATE:

What is your first memory of me?
What annoyed you about me when we were kids?

DATE:

If you have children, how did you choose their names?
Were there any alternate names you had in mind?

Do you like your name? If you could change
your name to anything else, what would it be?
What nicknames have you had over the years?

_____

_____

_____

_____

_____

_____

_____

_____

_____

_____

_____

_____

_____

_____

DATE:

What's the best piece of advice you've ever been given?
What advice do you wish you would have taken?

DATE:

Where do you see yourself in 5 years?
In 10? In 15?

DATE:

How do you want to spend the last years of your life? Do you want to live where you currently do or someplace else?

_____

_____

_____

_____

_____

_____

_____

_____

_____

_____

_____

Do you have any goals and dreams you still want to fulfill?

DATE:

What are the best memories you have
of our parents and of us as a family?

Do you believe in an afterlife?
Is so, what do you imagine it to be like?

DATE:

Did you like answering the questions in this book?
Is there anything else you want to add?

PHOTOGRAPHS & MEMORABILIA

PHOTOGRAPHS & MEMORABILIA

PHOTOGRAPHS & MEMORABILIA

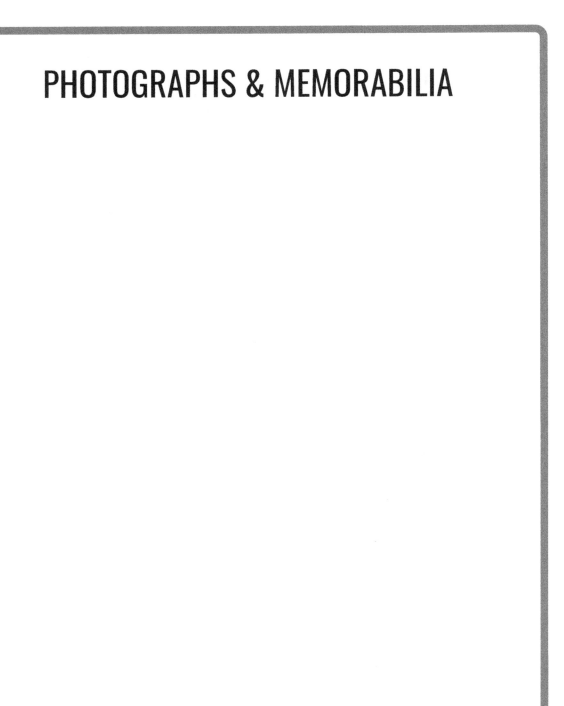

PHOTOGRAPHS & MEMORABILIA

PHOTOGRAPHS & MEMORABILIA

PHOTOGRAPHS & MEMORIBILIA

PHOTOGRAPHS & MEMORIBILIA

PHOTOGRAPHS & MEMORIBILIA

Made in the USA
Las Vegas, NV
15 December 2024

14342729R00057